MW01245592

THINGS TO MAKE
THE YEAR OF THE
INDIE AUTHORS
GREAT

B Alan Bourgeois

AWARD-WINNING AUTHOR
AWARD-WINNING SPEAKER
AUTHOR ADVOCATE

Year of the Indie Authors

Top Twelve Things to Make the Year of the Indie Authors Great

© B Alan Bourgeois 2023

merchantability or fitness for a particular purpose. The purchaser or reader of this book assumes complete responsibility for the use of these materials and information.

Any legal disputes arising from the use of this book shall be governed by the laws of the jurisdiction where the book was purchased, without regard to its conflict of law provisions, and shall be resolved exclusively in the courts of that jurisdiction.

ISBN: 978-1-7375239-8-7

Publisher: Bourgeois Media & Consulting (BourgeoisMedia.com)

BOURGEOIS
MEDIA & CONSULTING

Introduction

Here are the top 12 things authors can do to be actively involved and successful in the 2024 Year of the Indie Authors, that they can do year round.

By participating in the Year of the Indie Author program and utilizing these strategies, indie authors can gain more exposure, attract new readers, and ultimately achieve greater success in their writing careers.

For the purposes of this book and for the event, here is a definition of what an Indie Author is:

An indie author is typically defined as a self-published author who has chosen to forego traditional publishing methods in favor of taking full control of the publishing process, from writing to editing, formatting, cover design, and distribution. Indie authors may use online publishing platforms, such as Amazon's Kindle Direct Publishing or Barnes & Noble's Nook Press, to release their books in electronic and/or print formats. They are responsible for all aspects of their book's success, including marketing and promotion, and may rely on their own networks and social media platforms to build their audience. The term "indie" is short for "independent," reflecting the author's decision to work outside the traditional publishing industry.

We further define an Indie Author to be an author that is published by a traditional style publishing house that publishes less then 12 books per year. These publishers are considered to be small publisher, and also known as indie publishers.

Contents

1
Get Involved in Social Media Campaigns

Social media has become an integral part of our daily lives, with billions of people logging onto platforms like Facebook, Instagram, and Twitter every day. For indie authors, social media can be a powerful tool to connect with readers, build a following, and promote their work. In the 2024 Year of the Indie Author program, getting involved in social media campaigns is an important step towards success.

Social media campaigns are coordinated efforts by groups of people or organizations to promote a specific message, product, or cause. They often involve the use of a specific hashtag, which can be used to track the campaign's reach and engagement. In the context of the 2024 Year of the Indie Author program, social media campaigns will be used to promote indie authors and their work, and to encourage readers to discover and engage with new writers.

So, how can indie authors get involved in social media campaigns during the 2024 Year of the Indie Author program? Here are some tips:

1. Follow the program's social media accounts: The 2024 Year of the Indie Author program will likely have its own social media accounts on platforms like Twitter, Instagram, and Facebook. Make sure to follow these accounts to stay up-to-date on the latest news and events related to the program.

2. Participate in hashtag campaigns: Hashtag campaigns are a popular way to promote a message or cause on social media. During the 2024 Year of the Indie Author program, there may be specific hashtags that indie authors can use

to promote their work and connect with readers. Make sure to use these hashtags in your social media posts to participate in the campaign and increase your visibility.

3. Collaborate with other authors: Collaborating with other indie authors can help you expand your reach and attract new readers. You can collaborate on social media campaigns, joint promotions, or even create a joint hashtag to promote your work together.

4. Use social media to share your writing journey: Social media is a great platform to share your writing journey with your followers. Share updates on your writing process, sneak peeks of your work, and behind-the-scenes insights into your life as an author. This can help readers connect with you on a personal level and build a loyal following.

5. Engage with your followers: Social media is all about

engagement. Take the time to respond to comments, like and share posts from your followers, and participate in discussions related to your work. This can help you build a relationship with your followers and create a community around your work.

6.   Host giveaways or contests: Hosting a giveaway or contest on social media can be a fun way to engage with your followers and promote your work. You can give away copies of your book, offer exclusive content or merchandise, or even host a writing challenge to encourage readers to engage with your work.

Overall, getting involved in social media campaigns is an important step towards success as an indie author in the 2024 Year of the Indie Author program. By using social media to promote your work, connect with readers, and build a following, you can increase your visibility and attract new readers to your writing.

2
Participate in Online Events

The 2024 Year of the Indie Author is an initiative aimed at promoting independent authors and their work, and one of the key ways to achieve this goal is by participating in online events. With the rise of digital technology, there has been an increase in the number of virtual events, making it easier for authors to connect with readers from all over the world.

Online events provide a platform for authors to showcase their work, connect with readers, and build their brand. Here are some of the ways authors can participate in online events as part of the 2024 Year of the Indie Author program:

1.   Book fairs: Virtual book fairs are a great way to showcase your work and connect with readers. These events often feature author readings, book signings, and panel discussions.

Participating in a virtual book fair allows authors to reach a wider audience, and it provides an opportunity to network with other authors and industry professionals.

2.   Author panels: Author panels are a popular type of online event that allows authors to discuss their work and share their experiences with readers. Participating in an author panel provides an opportunity for authors to connect with readers who are interested in their genre and learn from other authors.

3.   Book clubs: Virtual book clubs provide a platform for authors to engage with readers who are interested in their work. By participating in a book club, authors can answer readers' questions, discuss their writing process, and gain valuable feedback.

4.   Writing workshops: Writing workshops are online events where authors can learn new skills and improve their craft. These events are

often led by experienced writers or industry professionals, and they provide an opportunity to connect with other writers and gain insights into the publishing industry.

5.   Author interviews: Author interviews are a great way to promote your work and connect with readers. These events allow authors to discuss their writing process, share their experiences, and promote their latest work.

Participating in online events as part of the 2024 Year of the Indie Author program provides a range of benefits for independent authors. By connecting with readers, building their brand, and networking with other authors and industry professionals, authors can increase their exposure and attract new readers. In addition, participating in online events provides an opportunity to learn from other authors and industry professionals and improve their craft.

To make the most of online events, authors should be proactive in promoting their participation. This can be achieved by sharing information about the event on social media, including details in email newsletters, and creating engaging content that promotes their participation.

In conclusion, participating in online events as part of the 2024 Year of the Indie Author program is an excellent way for independent authors to connect with readers and promote their work. By participating in book fairs, author panels, book clubs, writing workshops, and author interviews, authors can build their brand, network with other authors and industry professionals, and increase their exposure to potential readers.

3
Offer Special Promotions

Offering special promotions is a great way for indie authors to attract new readers and generate buzz around their work. As part of the 2024 Year of the Indie Author program, authors can take advantage of this tactic to increase their visibility and connect with potential readers.

Here are some tips on how indie authors can offer special promotions as part of the Year of the Indie Author program:

1.   Discounted Book Prices One effective way to attract new readers is to offer discounted prices on your books. This can be done through various channels, including Amazon, Barnes & Noble, and other online book retailers. For example, you can offer a discount code for readers to use when purchasing your

book on a specific platform. This can help incentivize readers to give your book a try and can also help boost your sales and rankings.

2.   Free eBooks

Offering free eBooks is another way to attract new readers and generate buzz around your work. You can offer a free eBook on a limited-time basis, either through your website or through an eBook retailer such as Amazon. This can be a great way to introduce new readers to your work and encourage them to check out your other titles.

3.   Signed Copies

Signed copies of your books can be a great way to offer a personal touch and make your readers feel special. You can offer signed copies through your website, through social media giveaways, or at book signings and other events. This can be especially effective for building relationships with your readers and encouraging them to share your work with others.

4.   Bundled Packages

Bundled packages can also be an effective way to attract new readers and generate sales. For example, you can bundle several of your books together and offer them at a discounted price. This can help readers discover more of your work and encourage them to become long-term fans.

5.   Limited Editions

Limited editions of your books can be a great way to create excitement and demand around your work. You can offer limited edition copies with special features such as bonus content, special covers, or unique packaging. This can help make your books more collectible and can also help you stand out from other authors in your genre.

In conclusion, offering special promotions is an effective way for indie authors to attract new readers and generate buzz around their work. By discounting book prices, offering free eBooks, signed copies, bundled packages, and limited editions, indie authors can increase their visibility and connect with potential readers. By participating in the 2024 Year of the Indie Author program, authors can take advantage of these tactics and build their readership and success.

4
Collaborate with Other Indie Authors

Collaboration is a powerful tool for indie authors looking to expand their reach and connect with new readers. By partnering with other independent authors, you can amplify your marketing efforts and tap into new audiences.

The 2024 Year of the Indie Author initiative offers an excellent opportunity for indie authors to collaborate with one another. The program is designed to bring independent authors together and provide them with a platform to showcase their work.

Here are some ways indie authors can collaborate with one another to make the most of the Year of the Indie Author initiative:

1. Co-author a book: Co-authoring a book with another indie author can be

a great way to expand your audience and reach new readers. You can collaborate on everything from the plot to the marketing strategy, and each bring your own unique perspective to the project.

2.   Cross-promote each other's work: Collaborating with other indie authors to cross-promote each other's work is another effective strategy. This can involve promoting each other's books on social media, mentioning each other's work in email newsletters, or even hosting joint giveaways.

3.   Participate in joint events: As part of the Year of the Indie Author program, there will be virtual events such as author panels and book fairs that indie authors can participate in. Partnering with other indie authors to participate in these events can help you reach a wider audience.

4.   Create a joint marketing campaign: Another way to collaborate with other indie authors is to create a joint marketing campaign. You can

work together to create a unified message and promote each other's work across multiple channels.

5.   Share resources: Indie authors often have limited resources, so sharing resources with other authors can be mutually beneficial. This can involve sharing editing or formatting services, or even pooling your resources to invest in joint advertising campaigns.

Collaborating with other indie authors can be a powerful way to reach new readers and build your audience. By working together, you can pool your resources, amplify your marketing efforts, and tap into new audiences. So if you're an indie author looking to make the most of the 2024 Year of the Indie Author initiative, consider collaborating with other independent authors to expand your reach and connect with new readers.

5
Build a Strong Author Platform

As an indie author, building a strong author platform is crucial to your success. Your platform is your online presence and the way you connect with your audience. In the 2024 Year of the Indie Author, building a strong author platform can be one of the most effective ways to attract new readers and build your brand. Here are some tips on how to build a strong author platform in the Year of the Indie Author.

1. Create a professional website Your website is your online hub and the first impression readers will have of you. It's essential to have a professional-looking website that showcases your work, your brand, and your personality. Make sure your website is user-friendly and easy to navigate. Include a bio, a list of your

books, and links to your social media profiles.

2.   Optimize your website for search engines

Search engine optimization (SEO) is the process of optimizing your website to rank higher in search engine results. When someone searches for your name or the genre you write in, you want your website to be at the top of the search results. To optimize your website, make sure your content is relevant, your keywords are strategically placed, and your website is mobile-friendly.

3.   Create a blog

Blogging is a great way to connect with your audience and showcase your expertise. Share your writing journey, writing tips, or behind-the-scenes glimpses into your life. Blogging can also help you establish yourself as an authority in your niche.

4.   Use social media strategically

Social media is a powerful tool for indie authors to connect with readers and promote their work. Choose the platforms that work best for you and your audience and use them strategically. Share snippets of your work, photos of your writing process, and behind-the-scenes glimpses into your life. Engage with your followers and build relationships with them.

5.   Build an email list

Email marketing is one of the most effective ways to connect with your audience and promote your work. Offer readers a freebie, such as a free book or a sneak peek into your next project, in exchange for their email address. Once you have their email address, you can send them updates, promotions, and other content that will keep them engaged with your brand.

6.   Create a podcast or a YouTube channel

If you're comfortable with speaking in front of a camera or a microphone, creating a podcast or a YouTube channel can be a great way to build your brand and connect with your audience. Share your writing journey, conduct interviews with other authors, or discuss writing topics that are important to your niche.

7. Offer valuable content

Your audience wants to hear from you, but they also want to get something of value. Offer them something they can't find anywhere else, such as exclusive content, behind-the-scenes glimpses into your life, or writing tips. The more valuable content you offer, the more engaged your audience will be.

In conclusion, building a strong author platform is essential for indie authors who want to succeed in the 2024 Year of the Indie Author. Create a professional website, optimize it for search engines, create a blog, use social media strategically, build an email list, create a podcast or a YouTube channel, and offer valuable content to your audience. By doing so, you can build your brand, attract new readers, and establish yourself as an authority in your niche.

6
Engage with Existing Readers

Engaging with existing readers is a critical aspect of building a successful career as an independent author. It not only helps you maintain a loyal readership but also attracts new readers who are interested in your work. In the 2024 Year of the Indie Author program, engaging with existing readers is more important than ever, as it can help you grow your readership and increase your exposure as an independent author.

Here are some tips for engaging with your existing readers:

1. Respond to comments and messages: Whenever someone leaves a comment on your blog or social media posts or sends you a message, make sure to respond promptly. This not only shows that you appreciate their support but also

helps you build a relationship with them.

2.   Use email newsletters: Email newsletters are a great way to keep in touch with your readers and inform them about your latest releases, events, and promotions. Make sure your newsletters are informative, engaging, and personalized to the interests of your readers.

3.   Offer exclusive content: Offer your existing readers exclusive content such as behind-the-scenes looks at your writing process, deleted scenes, or bonus stories. This not only rewards your existing readers but also gives them a reason to continue supporting you.

4.   Host reader events: Host events such as Q&A sessions, book clubs, or online book parties to engage with your readers directly. This not only helps you connect with your readers on a personal level but also encourages them to share your work with their friends and followers.

5.　Ask for feedback: Ask your existing readers for feedback on your work and incorporate their suggestions into your future writing. This not only shows that you value their opinion but also helps you improve your writing and attract new readers.

6.　Show appreciation: Show your appreciation for your existing readers by offering them special discounts or signed copies of your books. This not only rewards their loyalty but also encourages them to continue supporting you.

In conclusion, engaging with existing readers is an essential aspect of building a successful career as an independent author. By responding to comments and messages, using email newsletters, offering exclusive content, hosting reader events, asking for feedback, and showing appreciation, you can maintain a loyal readership and attract new readers interested in your work. In the 2024 Year of the Indie Author program, engaging with existing readers is more important than ever, as it can help you grow your readership and increase your exposure as an independent author.

7
Create Engaging and High-Quality Content

In the world of writing, content is king. As an indie author, your success depends on your ability to create high-quality, engaging content that resonates with readers. In the 2024 Year of the Indie Author, creating engaging and high-quality content is more important than ever, as the competition for readers' attention continues to grow.

So, what does it mean to create engaging and high-quality content as an indie author? Let's break it down.

Engaging Content

Engaging content is content that captures readers' attention and keeps them interested. This can be achieved in a number of ways, such as:

1.	Writing a compelling opening: The first few sentences of your book or blog post are crucial. They should hook the reader and make them want to keep reading.
2.	Creating relatable characters: Readers want to be able to connect with the characters in your story. Make sure your characters are well-developed and relatable.
3.	Adding conflict: Conflict is what drives a story forward. Make sure there is plenty of conflict in your writing to keep readers engaged.
4.	Using descriptive language: Use descriptive language to create vivid images in readers' minds. This will help them feel like they are a part of the story.

High-Quality Content

High-quality content is content that is well-written, error-free, and polished. Here are some tips for creating high-quality content:

1.   Edit, edit, edit: Take the time to edit your work carefully. Look for spelling and grammar errors, as well as inconsistencies in plot or character development.

2.   Use beta readers: Beta readers are a great resource for getting feedback on your writing. They can help you identify areas that need improvement and offer suggestions for how to make your writing better.

3.   Hire a professional editor: If you have the budget, consider hiring a professional editor to review your work. They can help you identify areas that need improvement and offer suggestions for how to make your writing better.

4.   Polish your writing: Take the time to polish your writing until it shines. This means paying attention to things like sentence structure, pacing, and dialogue.

In the 2024 Year of the Indie Author, creating engaging and high-quality content is more important than ever. By focusing on these elements, you can attract new readers and keep your existing fans engaged. Whether you are writing a novel, a blog post, or a social media update, remember that your content is the key to your success as an indie author.

8
Attend Book Fairs
and Festivals

Attending book fairs and festivals is a great way for indie authors to promote their work, meet new readers, and connect with other authors in the industry. In the 2024 Year of the Indie Author, participating in these events can be a key element to a successful marketing strategy.

Book fairs and festivals are usually held in cities around the world, and are open to the public. They can range from small-scale events to large, international book fairs that attract tens of thousands of visitors. These events offer a unique opportunity for indie authors to showcase their work and connect with readers in person.

Here are some tips for indie authors looking to attend book fairs and festivals in the 2024 Year of the Indie Author:

1. Research book fairs and festivals in your area: Look for events that are relevant to your genre and target audience. Many book fairs and festivals have websites with information on dates, venues, and how to register.

2. Plan your booth or table: If you plan to have a booth or table at the event, make sure to prepare materials such as business cards, bookmarks, and flyers. Consider creating a banner or poster that showcases your book covers and author brand.

3. Engage with visitors: Be prepared to engage with visitors and talk about your work. Have a brief elevator pitch ready that summarizes your book and what makes it unique.

4. Offer special promotions: Consider offering special promotions at the event, such as discounted book

prices or signed copies. This can help attract new readers and generate buzz around your work.

5. Network with other authors: Book fairs and festivals are also a great opportunity to network with other authors in the industry. Exchange contact information and consider collaborating on joint promotions or events in the future.

Attending book fairs and festivals can be a fun and rewarding experience for indie authors. It offers the opportunity to meet new readers, promote your work, and connect with others in the industry. By following these tips, you can make the most of your time at these events and increase your chances of success in the 2024 Year of the Indie Author.

9
Utilize Paid Advertising Platforms

As an indie author, it can be challenging to get your work in front of the right audience. While social media, email marketing, and other organic methods are effective, they can take time to gain traction. That's where paid advertising comes in.

In the 2024 Year of the Indie Author, utilizing paid advertising platforms can be a powerful tool to reach new readers and promote your work. Here are some tips on how to effectively utilize paid advertising:

1. Set a budget: Before diving into paid advertising, it's important to set a budget. Determine how much you are willing to spend on advertising and allocate it accordingly.

2.   Choose the right platform: There are a variety of advertising platforms available, each with its own benefits and drawbacks. Facebook, Instagram, Amazon, and Bookbub are just a few of the options available to indie authors. Research which platforms are most effective for your genre and audience.

3.   Target your audience: One of the biggest advantages of paid advertising is the ability to target specific audiences. Use the platform's targeting options to hone in on readers who are most likely to be interested in your work.

4.   Create compelling ad content: Your ad content should be eye-catching, informative, and memorable. Use high-quality images and concise, attention-grabbing copy to draw in potential readers.

5.   Monitor and adjust: Paid advertising can be a trial-and-error process. Monitor the performance of your ads and adjust as needed. Make

note of what is working and what isn't, and adjust your strategy accordingly.

6.   Consider collaborating with other authors: Collaborating with other indie authors on advertising campaigns can help to increase your reach and lower advertising costs. Partnering with authors who write in similar genres can help to attract the right audience.

7.   Don't forget about your landing page: Your ad may be effective at drawing readers in, but your landing page is what will ultimately sell your book. Make sure your landing page is professional, easy to navigate, and provides readers with all the information they need to make a purchase.

Paid advertising can be an effective way to reach new readers and promote your work. By setting a budget, choosing the right platform, targeting your audience, creating compelling ad content, monitoring and adjusting, collaborating with other authors, and optimizing your landing page, you can effectively utilize paid advertising to grow your readership during the 2024 Year of the Indie Author.

10
Offer Exclusive Content
or Bonuses to Readers

As an indie author, one of the most important things you can do to attract and retain readers is to offer them exclusive content or bonuses. This is especially important in the 2024 Year of the Indie Author, where the competition is likely to be fierce.

By offering exclusive content or bonuses, you can give readers an incentive to choose your work over that of other authors. This could include anything from exclusive short stories or bonus chapters to behind-the-scenes insights into your writing process or even signed copies of your books.

Here are some tips on how to offer exclusive content or bonuses to your readers:

1.   Make it valuable: Whatever you offer as exclusive content or bonus material should be something that readers will genuinely appreciate. Make sure it's something that adds value to their experience of your work and makes them feel like they're getting something extra special.

2.   Make it easy to access: Once you've created your exclusive content or bonus material, make sure it's easy for readers to access it. This could be as simple as including a link in your book or on your website, or setting up a special landing page for readers to access.

3.   Use it as a marketing tool: Offering exclusive content or bonuses can be a powerful marketing tool. Use it to entice new readers to check out your work, or to encourage existing readers to leave reviews or spread the word about your books.

4.   Keep it fresh: To keep readers engaged and coming back for more, it's important to keep your exclusive

content or bonuses fresh and interesting. Consider offering new content or bonuses on a regular basis, or tying them into specific events or promotions.

5. Make it interactive: To really engage readers, consider making your exclusive content or bonuses interactive. This could include things like live Q&A sessions, online book clubs, or even personalized feedback on their writing.

Overall, offering exclusive content or bonuses to your readers is a great way to build a loyal fanbase and stand out from the crowd in the 2024 Year of the Indie Author. By making your content valuable, easy to access, and fresh, and using it as a marketing and engagement tool, you can help ensure the success of your indie author career.

11
Host Giveaways
or Contests

In the ever-evolving world of publishing, indie authors are constantly seeking new and innovative ways to attract and engage readers. One strategy that has proven to be successful is hosting giveaways or contests. This technique not only generates buzz around an author's work but also provides an opportunity to interact with readers and potentially attract new fans. In this article, we will explore how indie authors can use giveaways and contests to their advantage in the 2024 Year of the Indie Author.

Benefits of hosting giveaways and contests

One of the main benefits of hosting giveaways or contests is the potential to increase engagement with readers. By offering a prize or reward for participation, authors can encourage readers to interact with their work and potentially attract new fans. Additionally, hosting giveaways and contests can generate buzz around an author's work and increase visibility on social media platforms.

Another benefit of hosting giveaways and contests is the opportunity to receive feedback from readers. Authors can ask participants to leave reviews or provide feedback on their work, which can be used to improve future projects. How to host a successful giveaway or contest

1. Set clear goals: Before hosting a giveaway or contest, authors should have a clear understanding of what they hope to achieve. This could include increasing social media followers, generating book reviews, or increasing sales. By setting clear goals, authors can tailor their

giveaway or contest to best achieve these objectives.

2. Determine the prize: The prize offered should be relevant to the author's work and appeal to their target audience. This could include signed copies of their book, merchandise related to the book's theme, or a gift card to a popular retailer.

3. Choose the platform: There are numerous platforms available for hosting giveaways and contests, including social media, email newsletters, and author websites. Authors should choose the platform that best aligns with their goals and target audience.

4. Promote the giveaway or contest: To maximize participation, authors should promote the giveaway or contest through their website, social media, and email list. They can also collaborate with other authors or bloggers to increase visibility.

5. Monitor and follow up: After the giveaway or contest ends, authors should monitor and follow up with participants. This could include announcing the winner publicly, sending a thank-you email to participants, or requesting feedback on their experience.

Examples of successful giveaways and contests

- A romance author hosted a giveaway where participants could win a personalized love letter from the main character of their book. To enter, participants had to leave a review on Amazon or Goodreads.
- A mystery author hosted a scavenger hunt contest on social media where participants had to find clues related to their book. The winner received a signed copy of the book and a gift card.
- A fantasy author hosted a fan art contest where participants could submit their own artwork inspired by

the author's book. The winner received a signed copy of the book and a personalized thank-you note.

In conclusion, hosting giveaways and contests can be a powerful tool for indie authors looking to increase engagement and attract new fans. By setting clear goals, choosing the right prize, promoting through the right platform, and following up with participants, authors can maximize the impact of their giveaway or contest.

12
Build Relationships with Book Bloggers and Bookstagrammers

In the 2024 Year of the Indie Author, building relationships with book bloggers and bookstagrammers can be a valuable strategy for indie authors to gain exposure and attract new readers. These influencers have dedicated followings who trust their opinions and recommendations, making them a powerful tool for promoting books.

Book bloggers are individuals who write reviews and share recommendations of books they have read on their personal blogs or websites. They often have niche interests and audiences, such as young adult fiction, romance novels, or non-fiction works. Bookstagrammers, on the other hand, are Instagram users who specialize in sharing visually appealing photos of books, often accompanied by reviews or recommendations in the captions.

Here are some ways indie authors can build relationships with book bloggers and bookstagrammers:

1. Research and identify relevant influencers: Start by researching book bloggers and bookstagrammers who are interested in your genre or niche. Look for influencers who have a significant following and engagement with their audience.

2. Reach out and introduce yourself: Once you have identified relevant influencers, reach out to them via email or direct message on social media. Introduce yourself and your work and express your interest in working together.

3. Offer a review copy of your book: Many book bloggers and bookstagrammers are happy to receive review copies of books. Offer to send them a digital or physical copy of your book in exchange for an

honest review or feature on their platform.

4. Participate in blog tours or Instagram challenges: Many book bloggers and bookstagrammers organize blog tours or Instagram challenges, where they feature a group of authors or books around a specific theme or topic. Participating in these events can be a great way to build relationships with influencers and gain exposure for your work.

5. Share their content and engage with them: Building a relationship with influencers is a two-way street. Share their content on your own social media platforms and engage with their posts by commenting and liking. This can help establish a relationship and encourage them to support your work in return.

6. Offer exclusive content or interviews: Consider offering book bloggers and bookstagrammers exclusive content or interviews with you as an author. This can help them

create unique and valuable content for their followers while giving you additional exposure.

In conclusion, building relationships with book bloggers and bookstagrammers can be a valuable strategy for indie authors in the 2024 Year of the Indie Author. By identifying relevant influencers, offering review copies of your book, participating in blog tours and Instagram challenges, sharing their content and engaging with them, and offering exclusive content or interviews, indie authors can build relationships with influencers and gain exposure for their work.

What is the Definition of a Bookstagrammer?

A bookstagrammer is someone who uses the social media platform Instagram to share their love of books with their followers. They typically post photos of books, bookshelves, and reading nooks, along with reviews and recommendations. Bookstagrammers often have large followings and use their platform to engage with other book lovers, authors, and publishers.

Bookstagrammers are an important part of the book industry, as they can have a significant influence on what books their followers choose to read. They may also participate in book clubs, read-a-thons, and other book-related events on Instagram, which can further increase their reach.

To work with bookstagrammers as an author, it is important to build relationships with them by engaging with their content, commenting on their posts, and sharing their content with your own followers. You can also reach out to them to offer review copies of your book or to collaborate on a book-related event or promotion.

When working with bookstagrammers, it is important to be respectful of their time and effort. Bookstagrammers often put a lot of work into creating their content, so it is important to offer them something of value in return, such as a free book or exclusive content. By building strong relationships with bookstagrammers, authors can tap into their large followings and gain more exposure for their work.

Bonus Content
Being Involved with
a Tight Budget

A lot of what has been written so far has
a certain time and financial commitment
to it. The flowing is a less costly way to
participate in the 2024 Year of the Indie
Authors that can along with the above,
help an author year-round.

Participating in the 2024 Year of the
Indie Authors can be an excellent way to
gain exposure and attract new readers
to your work as an independent author.
However, as an author with limited time
and funds, it can be challenging to
participate in various events and
promotions. Here are some tips on how
to participate in the Year of the Indie
Authors program effectively:

1. Utilize social media: Social media
is a great way to promote your work
and connect with potential readers.
Take advantage of free social media

platforms like Twitter, Instagram, and Facebook to promote your books, participate in online events, and engage with other indie authors.

2.   Offer free samples: Give readers a taste of your writing by offering free samples of your work. This could include the first chapter of your book or a short story. Free samples can help entice readers to purchase your book and can be a great way to build your email list.

3.   Engage with your readers: Engage with your readers through email newsletters, social media, or other means. Encourage them to share your work with their friends and followers. Ask for reviews and feedback to help improve your writing and boost your online presence.

4.   Partner with other indie authors: Partnering with other indie authors can help you reach a wider audience and expand your reach. Collaborate on social media campaigns, online

events, or joint promotions to reach a broader audience.

5.   Attend local events: Participate in local events such as book clubs or library events. These events are a great way to connect with readers in your community and promote your work.

6.   Focus on your author platform: Building a strong author platform is key to attracting new readers. Make sure your website, social media profiles, and other online presence are up-to-date and engaging. Use your platform to showcase your work and connect with potential readers.

7.   Offer special promotions: As part of the Year of the Indie Author program, authors can offer special promotions such as discounted book prices, free eBooks, or signed copies of their books. These promotions can help attract new readers and generate buzz around your work.

8.   Utilize free marketing tools: There are many free marketing tools

available online that you can use to promote your work. These include book listing sites, social media scheduling tools, and email marketing services.

9.

In conclusion, participating in the 2024 Year of the Indie Authors program doesn't have to be expensive or time-consuming. By utilizing social media, offering free samples, engaging with readers, partnering with other indie authors, attending local events, focusing on your author platform, offering special promotions, and utilizing free marketing tools, indie authors with limited time and funds can effectively participate in the program and attract new readers to their work.

B Alan Bourgeois began his writing career at the age of 12, writing screenplays for the Adam-12 show. Despite not submitting them for review, this experience sparked his passion for writing. However, he followed the advice of his generation and pursued higher education to secure a stable job. It wasn't until 1989, after taking a writing class at a community college, that Bourgeois wrote a short story that was published. Since then, he has written over 48 short stories and published more than 10 books, including the award-winning spiritual thriller "Extinguishing the Light."

Bourgeois has become a champion for authors and founded the Texas Authors Association in 2011 to help Texas authors better market and sell their books. This led to the creation of the Texas Authors Institute of History, Inc., and the first online museum of its kind, the Texas Authors Institute. He also created several short story contests and fundraising programs for Texas students and consolidated small-town book festivals into the Lone Star Festival, promoting Texas authors, musicians, artists, and filmmakers. In 2016, he founded the Authors Marketing Event and added a Certification program in 2017, allowing attendees to gain accreditation for their hard work in learning book marketing. His recent focus has been on assisting authors of all levels to become successful Authorpreneurs through the Authors School of Business, which offers programs to help grow their careers. He is currently working with NFTs for authors to help them increase their income channels.

Click here to schedule a FREE 15 min consultation

Click here for a more detailed biography of Alan

Click here for Testimonials

Top Ten Book Series and Other Books by the Author

Available at Your Favorite Bookstore

Top Ten Mistakes Authors Make when Creating a Book Cover

TOP TEN
MISTAKES
AUTHORS MAKE
IN CREATING A
BOOK COVER

B. Alan Bourgeois

AWARD-WINNING AUTHOR
AWARD-WINNING SPEAKER
AUTHOR ADVOCATE

LEARN HOW TO
AVOID THE
MISTAKES

Your book cover is your first impression. Don't let a lackluster design hold you back. "Top Ten Mistakes Authors Make When Creating a Book Cover" is your comprehensive guide to avoid common pitfalls and create a cover that truly represents your work. Discover practical tips on how to choose the right colors, fonts, and design, and avoid using low-quality images and cluttered layouts. With real-world examples and expert advice, this book will help you create a cover that grabs readers' attention and leads to more sales.

Don't let a poorly designed book cover hold you back from success. Whether you're self-publishing or working with a traditional publisher, "Top Ten Mistakes Authors Make When Creating a Book

Cover" is a must-read. Order your copy today and take your book to the next level!

TOP TEN
THINGS TO
CONSIDER FOR
A GREAT
SALES PITCH

B Alan Bourgeois

AWARD WINNING AUTHOR
AWARD WINNING SPEAKER
AUTHOR ADVOCATE

LEARN HOW TO
AVOID THE
MISTAKES

Top Ten Things to Consider for a Great Sales Pitch

Are you struggling to create a sales pitch that really resonates with your audience? Look no further than "Top Ten Things to Consider for a Great Sales Pitch"! This ultimate guide will take you through the ten most important steps to creating a sales pitch that will grab your target audience's attention and convince them to buy your book.

Learn how to identify your target audience and highlight the unique value of your book, using emotional language to connect with readers on a personal level. Be concise and to the point, and practice your pitch until you can deliver it smoothly and confidently. Incorporate social proof and visuals to make your pitch more compelling, and tailor it to the specific interests and needs of your audience.

Above all, be authentic and genuine. With the help of "Top Ten Things to Consider for a Great Sales Pitch", you'll be able to create a sales pitch that not only sells your book, but also connects with your audience and builds a loyal fan base. Don't miss out on this essential resource for any author looking to take their sales pitch to the next level!

Top Ten Publishing Issues Authors Deal With

Are you an aspiring author struggling with the daunting publishing process? Look no further than "Top Ten Publishing Issues Authors Deal With." This essential guide tackles the most common challenges writers face, including rejection, editing, marketing, distribution, audience building, time management, and legal issues like copyright infringement. Our expert advice will help you navigate the complex world of publishing and achieve success. Plus, we'll guide you through the formatting process, even for ebooks that need to work on multiple devices and software. Don't let self-doubt and imposter syndrome hinder your progress - get the knowledge you need to thrive in the publishing world. Order your copy of "Top Ten Publishing Issues Authors Deal With" today.

Top Ten Marketing Materials an Author Should Use

"Top Ten Marketing Items Authors Should Use" is the ultimate guide for authors who want to boost book sales and increase visibility. Discover the top ten marketing materials every author should use, including eye-catching bookmarks, business cards, posters, and book trailers. You'll also learn insider tips on how to write an attention-grabbing press release and build an author website that attracts readers and media attention. Plus, social media marketing, author blogging, email newsletters, and swag creation strategies will help you connect with readers, build your author brand, and create a loyal fan base. Don't let your book languish in obscurity - get your copy of "Top Ten Marketing Items Authors Should Use" today and take the first step towards successful book promotion!

TOP TEN
MISTAKES
AUTHORS MAKE
MARKETING THEIR
BOOKS

B Alan Bourgeois
AWARD-WINNING AUTHOR &
AWARD-WINNING SPEAKER
AUTHOR ADVOCATE

LEARN HOW TO
AVOID THE
MISTAKES

Top Ten Mistakes an Author Makes Marketing Their Books

Are you an author struggling to make a name for yourself in the crowded world of book marketing? Do you want to avoid the most common mistakes that authors make when promoting their books? Then look no further than "Top 10 Mistakes Authors Make Marketing Their Books" by B Alan Bourgeois.

As an award-winning author and author advocate with years of experience in the publishing industry, Bourgeois has seen it all when it comes to book marketing. In this insightful guide, he shares the top 10 mistakes that authors make and provides practical advice on how to avoid them.

Whether you're a first-time author or a seasoned pro, "Top 10 Mistakes Authors Make Marketing Their Books" is the essential guide for taking your book marketing to the next level. With Bourgeois's expert guidance, you'll learn how to identify your target audience, build a strong online presence, engage with readers, and leverage book reviews to increase sales.

Don't let common marketing mistakes hold you back from the success you deserve. Get your copy of "Top 10 Mistakes Authors Make Marketing Their Books" today and start marketing your book like a pro!

Top Ten Mistakes Authors Make During an Interview

Are you tired of stumbling through interviews, leaving the audience uninterested and disengaged? Do you struggle with staying focused and concise when answering tough questions? Look no further!

Our book provides you with the top ten mistakes authors commonly make at interviews and gives you practical tips on how to avoid them. From preparing adequately by researching the interviewer and their audience, to staying authentic and avoiding complex jargon, we cover it all.

Don't let your lack of enthusiasm or defensiveness turn off your audience. Instead, learn how to show genuine interest in your topic and stay calm during challenging questions. And most importantly, don't forget to thank your interviewer and audience for their time and attention - it can make all the difference in leaving a positive impression.

So, are you ready to improve your interview skills and leave a lasting impact on your audience? Get your copy of "Top Ten Mistakes Authors Do at Interviews" today!

Top Ten Mistakes Authors Make Presenting at Events

Are you an author struggling to present at events? "Top Ten Mistakes Authors Make Presenting at Events" is here to help you avoid common pitfalls and present your best self. Learn how to tailor your presentation to the audience's needs, engage with them effectively, promote your book without being pushy, and more!

With this ultimate guide, you'll avoid going off-topic, losing your audience's attention, and being dull and uninteresting. Practice and rehearse your presentation to deliver it smoothly and confidently. Get your copy of "Top Ten Mistakes Authors Make Presenting at Events" today and make the most of every event you attend!

Top Ten AI Programs Apps Authors Should Use

Attention all writers and authors! Are you looking for ways to improve your writing, stay organized, and streamline your workflow? Look no further than our latest book "Top Ten AI programs/Apps a writer/author should use". In this book, we have compiled a list of the top ten AI programs and apps that will help you with your writing, marketing, and workflow. From Grammarly and ProWritingAid to Hemingway and Dragon Dictation, these programs will help you write a great book.

Although the author has not used all of the programs listed, this list was compiled in 2023 from various sources and provides valuable insight into the most effective AI tools for writers and authors. Keep in mind that the AI community is constantly developing new resources and programs, so this list may not be the most up-to-date.

Don't miss out on the opportunity to improve your writing and streamline your workflow. Order "Top Ten AI programs/Apps a writer/author should use" now and start using these powerful tools to produce your best work.

TOP TEN
ADVANTAGES
INDIE AUTHORS
HAVE OVER
TRADITIONAL
AUTHORS

B Alan Bourgeois
AWARD-WINNING AUTHOR
AWARD-WINNING SPEAKER
AUTHOR ADVOCATE

EMBRACE YOUR
FINANCIAL
RECOURSES & GIFTS

Top Ten Advantages Indie Authors Have Over Traditional Authors

"Top Ten Advantages Indie Authors Have over Traditional" is the ultimate guide for authors looking to take control of their publishing process. With complete control over everything from writing to distribution, independent authors have more flexibility and creative control over their work.

This book highlights the benefits of indie publishing, including higher royalties, faster publishing timelines, the ability to target niche markets, and global distribution through online retailers. If you want more control over your book's content and the ability to reach readers worldwide, "Top Ten Advantages Indie Authors Have over Traditional" is a must-read. Get your copy today and start your journey towards independent publishing success!

Top Ten Pieces of Advice from an Author Advocate & Consultant

"Top Ten Pieces of Advice from an Author Advocate & Consultant" is the ultimate guide for aspiring writers. Learn from an experienced author consultant and advocate and take your writing career to the next level. From building an author platform to developing a marketing plan, this book offers invaluable insights and practical tips to help you achieve your writing goals and make your work stand out. Start your journey to becoming a successful author today by purchasing this must-have resource.

Top Twelve Things to Make the Year of the Indie Authors Great

Are you an indie author looking to make 2024 a great year for your writing career? Then look no further than the book "Top Twelve Things to Make the Year of the Indie Authors Great." This book offers valuable insights into the top 12 things that could make 2024 a great year for indie authors to gain more readers.

With increased acceptance of self-publishing and better distribution channels, indie authors have more options than ever before to reach a wider audience. Additionally, the rise of social media platforms and digital marketing offers affordable ways for authors to connect with readers and promote their work.

But that's not all. The book also covers the importance of collaborating with other authors, the increasing popularity of audiobooks, and the need for more diverse representation in literature. And for those looking to improve their writing skills and production quality, the book offers insights into the better tools and resources available to indie authors.

Finally, the book covers opportunities for indie authors to engage with their readers, showcase their work at book festivals and online events, and collaborate with traditional publishers. In short, "Top Twelve Things to Make the Year of the Indie Authors Great" is a must-read for any indie author looking to take their writing career to the next level in 2024.

100+ Questions a Writer/Author Should Ask

Looking to take your writing career to the next level? Look no further than "100+ Questions a Writer/Author Should Ask"! With over 100 questions curated by Award-Winning Author & Speaker B Alan Bourgeois, the founder and CEO of the Authors School of Business, this book is a must-have for any aspiring or established writer. Bourgeois, a seasoned publisher, author advocate, and educator, brings his wealth of experience to the table to help you better understand the publishing world and succeed in your career. Don't miss out on this valuable resource.

Authors' Revolution Workbook

Welcome to the Speakers Companion Workbook. This workbook is a continuous transforming workbook to help Authors better understand the cost of being an Author in today's publishing world.

The author will review all the hidden cost of being a published author in todays world. In addition, he reviews a variety of companies and organizations that are available to help an author succeed.

The initial workbook in the form of an eBook is free to anyone who attends one of my speaking engagements. Updates can be purchased through my website at http://BourgeoisMedia.com . We encourage Authors to submit information and updates to us so that

we can continue to create a healthy and positive revolution that brings more financial security to each author who wants to earn their fair share from the works they have created. You may submit your comments and praise to us directly via email at
BourgeoisMedia@outlook.com

Earn your Certification at the event, or virtually at
http://AuthorsSchoolofBusiness.com

ASB is the first and only organization to offer certification in book marketing.

Join us—Why? Simple, NO ONE Does What We Do!

Three Kinds of Self-publishing Author

      1. The Self-Publishers

      2. The Indie Authors

      3. The Authorpreneurs

Authors School of Business is the only One-Stop program that helps   authors from Pre-Publishing, Publishing, Marketing and Sales. Each program is

$14.95 per month or get two free months when paid annual dues $149.50 in full.

Beginners
Tailored for aspiring writers who dream of becoming published authors, our program is designed to help them grow with confidence and understanding about the publishing world. We provide the knowledge and tools to position their book in a more successful position for publication and marketing, empowering them to achieve their publishing goals.

Intermediate
Tailored for published authors who are looking to gain a deep understanding of book marketing concepts and get involved in festivals, events, and other programs to promote their book, this program is designed to give them that

extra edge in their book promotion efforts.

Advanced

The purpose of this program is to assist published authors in gaining a deeper understanding of advanced book marketing techniques. It is tailored for authors who are already published and are looking to enhance their marketing strategies to achieve greater success. The program offers advanced modules and concepts to empower authors with the knowledge and tools needed to excel in their book marketing efforts.

The following is everything that our Basic subscription service includes. Notices of new and exciting events that we create to help you market and sell your books are shared with subscribers as they become available.

- Participation in the DEAR Texas/DEAR Indie events – Book Festivals, Library Conferences, etc.

- ASB Author Showcase Interview - No Less the two times in a calendar year. The show is recorded live and then distributed as an audio podcast on most systems, including iHeart Radio. Video recordings are on YouTube. An additional marketing package authors can use on their social media system is available.

- Access to the Subscribers Only section of this website which contains articles, links, and connections to a variety of items and services to help you grow in marketing and selling your books.

- Access to all previous AME videos through our on-line campus. (40+ videos for beginners, intermediate and advanced authors.

- Discount on the Authors Marketing Event registration – an annual event held in September each year where authors and professionals join together to share valuable knowledge and insights on how to better market and sell books.

- Major discounts with our sponsors and other related industry businesses and organizations to help you save money.

- Access to our YouTube channel to promote interviews, readings, etc., of you and your books

- Newsletters with the latest information with informative articles to help you succeed

- Retail Store that includes images of book covers, and other related items from Authors on clothing, promotional items, that an author can sell or purchase. Students of ASB pay NO Set Up Fee to have their merchandise in the store, plus they earn up to 80% of the sale.

- Listing and ability to sell your book(s), and NFTs on our bookstore website http://B4R.Store